Dying To Be Reborn

Understanding Your Soul's Journey

Tiffany Ruiz, M.Msc.

Tiffany Ruiz, M.Msc.

. Copyright © 2017 Tiffany Ruiz, M.Msc.

All rights reserved.

Warning – Disclaimer

The purpose of this book is to educae and entertain. The author does not guarantee that anyone following the techniques, suggestions, tips, ideas, or strategies will become successful or cure any ailments either physical or mental. The author shall have neither liability nor responsibility to anyone with respect to any loss or damage caused, or alleged o be caused, directly or indirectly by the information contained in this book

ISBN-13: 978-1542554558

ISBN-10: 1542554551

DEDICATION

For my mom, Cheryl.
Thank you for all of the life lessons you have taught me. I pray your next life is pain free and full of love.

Contents

Introduction 2

Is There an Afterlife? 4

    Religion and the Afterlife 9

    Miguel 16

Soul and Consciousness 23

    Spirit 25

    Soul 29

    The Science 33

Why Reincarnate 43

    Why Don't We Remember? 50

    Why do kids remember past lives easier than adults? 55

    Do We Transmigrate to other species? 59

    How can I remember my own past life? 62

Lessons and Resolutions 67

    Connecting with Soul Groups 67

    Behaviors 72

Body Syndromes 78

Birth Marks / Birth Defects 81

Your Own Past Life Recall 89

The Restaurant 96

Why Reincarnation Matters 98

ACKNOWLEDGMENTS

Without my family, and their suppot of my crazy ideas, none of his would be possible. My husband, Adrian. My kids, Adrian, Azsa, and Anthony. Thank you so much for supporting me and my dreams. I love you all, more than words.

Dying To Be Reborn

Tiffany Ruiz, M.Msc.

Introduction

My mind is down there somewhere as I fly above the badlands of New Mexico
I can't explain why I should know the very trail he rode back to El Paso
Can it be that man can disappear from life and live another time
And does the mystery deepen 'cause you think that you yourself lived in that other time

Somewhere in my deepest thoughts familiar scenes and memories unfold
These wild and unexplained emotions that I've had so long, but I have never told
Like everytime I fly up through the heavens and I see you there below
I get the feeling sometime in another world I lived in El Paso

Marty Robbins

El Paso City

If my mom were alive, she would tell you I was a clingy child. She would tell you I cried and cried and never wanted to be put down.

When I was five years old I had a nightmare that was so real and so vivid that I remember it to this day as if it just happened.

I would ask my mom about places we had been together and she would laugh and say we never had been there.

When I asked her about my many, many birthmarks she would tell me that is where an angel had kissed me. I knew better.

I knew this was not my first life and at nine years old, I began my search for answers.

What happens when we die?
Do we reincarnate?
Why did I believe I had been somewhere my mom said I had never been?
Why did I have such a strong connection with certain places and time periods?

The more I searched, the more questions I had. There was a lot of information about case studies, but not a lot out there about the why and how. I searched high and low for the answers to my questions.

This book is the result of my search. It is a simple, no frills, down to earth, and straight to the point compilation of my 30 years of research about reincarnation. My hope is that it resonates with you, and you begin to remember your soul's own unique journey.

Tiffany Ruiz, M.Msc.

Is There an Afterlife?

What happens when we die? It is a subject that has fascinated humans for millennia. It is used as the foundation for all religions because without an afterlife, there would be no reason for believing in a higher power. It is used as the fundamental reasoning for those who do not believe in any form of a higher power; there is no afterlife and therefore, no God. There are hundreds, if not thousands, of books dedicated to the subject. What happens to "us" when we die is a subject that both fascinates us, and terrifies us.

For many who believe we live on after death, where we go is wholly dependent on the actions we take in our daily lives. This is the thread of commonality among all beliefs. If we have not lived a righteous and good life, we will go to place that is uncomfortable and difficult. We will find ourselves in a place that is filled with light and love if we have followed the Golden Rule. For those who do not believe in a higher power, we simply cease to exist.

For sceptics, the main argument is that we simply cannot know what happens to us after we die because none of us have died yet. This is a solid and valid point. Even so, the vast majority of people believe that we live on after we die in a spirit form. Proponents of life after death cite faith as their number one reason for believing. Many faiths seek to "save" an individual's soul by proselytizing to them. Sometimes they seek to "prove" life after death by recounting stories of people who have been on the brink of death, or who have died, and have been "brought back". They feel they are doing a good deed by spreading the belief that we all will go to a terrible place if we do not convert our faith.

There are few topics that create such a heated debate not only among non-believers and believers, but among believers themselves. Even among the believers of life after death there is dissention about what actually happens and where we really go. Many believe religion itself is about a belief in a Higher Power, notably God. It is not. It is about the afterlife and where we go when we rejoin the Creator or whatever name you have for a higher being. It is this piece of religion that is responsible for family feuds, lovers being kept apart, hundreds of wars, and even decisions about how a country is governed.

How can a topic that each and every one of us will have to face one day be the cause of so much heartache and misery? I'm not talking about the pain we experience when we lose a loved one. I'm talking about the friction our beliefs cause. For some, I believe, it is a true love of humanity. For others, it is an exercise of power.

The afterlife was a prominent and driving force for most ancient of civilizations. Recently, a grave was unearthed of a shamanic woman in Israel. The grave, dated 12,000 years ago, contained an eagle wing, a leopard bone, and another person's foot. Such items indicate the people of this culture believed the deceased needed these items with them after their physical bodies have died. What is the significance of these items and did these cultures also believe that what actions they took while living would have a profound impact on their final destination?

Dying To Be Reborn

Evidence of intentional burials can be traced back as far as 130,000 years to the Neanderthals. A man, of about 45 years, a woman, two children and three infants are found buried together in individual graves in La Farrassie. Stones with artificial impressions marked the graves and small pits containing flint tools and animal bones were also found. It is believed these items provided protection in the afterlife. Additionally, pits with burned animal bones and other material indicate a feast, presumably by family and clan members, prior to the final internment.

Because these graves and others like them are prehistoric, we cannot say for certain what the meanings are behind the objects found in the gravesites. We are only able to speculate based on our own ritualistic practices and the practices of recorded ancient civilization. What we have learned is that there are just as many different burial practices as there are beliefs about the afterlife and how we bury our dead is directly related to what we think will happen when we pass on from this world.

Despite the vast differences in burial practices we can discern from many of the religious texts from various civilizations that there are, at the very least, some common threads. There is a concept of a soul, the life force which survives after our physical bodies die. There is also the recurring theme of judgement, did we perform just and righteous acts while alive. Learning lessons seems to also be commonplace when reviewing afterlife concepts. Sometimes these lessons are learned while living in a physical body and other times the lessons need to be learned while in the afterlife. Most notably is the concept of a physical place where we reside, depending on the acts we performed while living.

Religion and the Afterlife

Many devout Christians would be stunned to learn that their own ideas of the afterlife, specifically the Heaven and Hell concept itself, do not originate from the bible. In fact, any mention of Heaven contained within the bible refers to a Kingdom of Heaven within oneself. All other mentions of the afterlife discuss resurrection and the lack thereof. Even verses relating to the death of Christ fail to describe the modern Christian concept of heaven, only recounting that Christ died for our sins. Likewise, only one verse in the bible, Revelations 14:11, describes our modern belief of what Hell would be like.

Our modern interpretations of Heaven and Hell can be traced back to early cultures and their "myths". There are stark differences to be sure. These differences are most apparent when reviewing who is admitted into the "good" place and who isn't. Looking at the overall concept of the two destinations (and sometimes three) however, it becomes obvious that Christianity does not hold the monopoly on heaven, hell, or the afterlife.

After death, Ancient Egyptians had to pass

through the gates of Duat. After having correctly named the guardians of the gate they were then subject to a weighing of the heart ceremony. It was at this time the deceased received a review of their time spent on earth and was judged on his or her actions. If the heart was too light (you let people walk all over you) or too heavy (you walked all over other people), you were banished to oblivion by being eaten by a crocodile-like God. If your heart weighed equally with Ma'at, your Ba and Ka (spirit and soul) were united as Akh and you were allowed to spend the rest of eternity with Osiris in a place that was beautiful and peaceful, sailing with him every day on his barge.

    Ancient Greeks believed that once you die, you travel to the underworld ruled by Hades. If you had the fare (two coins) you were allowed to sail on the five rivers surrounding the Underworld to the Gates of Hades' Palace. Here, you would pass through the gates guarded by a three-headed dog. If you were truly deceased, you were allowed to enter. If you were not dead, you were devoured by the guardian of the gate. Once inside, three Guardians passed judgement on your deeds while alive. If you were really good, you got to go to the Elysian

Fields, and if you were really really good you were allowed to reside with the Gods. If you were not good, you were sent to a place where you were tortured for all of eternity as punishment for your deeds while on earth.

Muslims believe there will be a Day of Judgement in which God himself will weigh the deeds of the deceased. If you performed more good deeds than bad you were admitted into Heaven and allowed to pass through one of eight gates (depending on your deeds). If you performed more bad deeds, or if you rejected Allah as the one true God, you were sentenced to eternal damnation and torture. The Quran provides vivid descriptions of both Heaven and Hell. Heaven, according to the Quran, is a place of tranquility with gardens and rivers, you will be reunited with family and loved ones, and you will always be in the sight of God. Hell is described as a place of eternal fire, pestilence, and torture.

Although no solid description of judgement day for Christians can be found in the Bible, we can recount what we know through various bible verses and stories that have been told to us by our Sunday school teachers. When we die, we will meet St. Peter at the "pearly gates" (12 gates made of pearl according to Revelations). St.

Peter will review his book of names to determine if we are admitted. If our name is listed in the book of life, we are allowed to enter into Heaven where there is no need for the sun or the moon and we live out our days in eternal bliss, never thirsting, and surrounded by our family and friends. However, if our name is not listed we will be sent straight to Hell for eternal damnation. It is also believed that if you confessed your sins prior to death all transgressions would be forgiven because God allowed his son to die to save all of humanity.

Judaic traditions believe in a final judgement as well. If you obeyed the 7 laws of Noah, regardless of your religion, you were allowed to live on in paradise. Failing to follow these rules and performing bad deeds meant you were sent to a place called Gahanna for purification. Descriptions of Gahanna are very similar to the Christian description of a fiery hell. The most wicked of deeds meant you were tortured in Gahanna and ultimately destroyed completely.

We can see from the basic views of the afterlife above that they all have common themes: a judgement of our actions, gates or gateways, a paradise-like place, and a place of torture and pain. But, what do eastern religions have to say about the afterlife? We find those stories and ideas are also similar in nature.

Chinese traditions believe that we will be taken to the god of moats where a review of our life will take place. From there, depending once again on our actions during our lifetime, we will be sent to one of the Buddhists paradises, to the dwelling place of immortals, or to the tenth court of hell for rebirth of our soul. Sinners are sent to the base of Mount Meru after 49 days for punishment in one or more levels of hell. Once punishment is complete, and lessons learned, the soul is given a drink of the elixir of oblivion and sent back to earth for reincarnation to try again by way of a river.

Early texts related to Hinduism, namely the Vedic texts, indicate that different people are sent different places after death. However, there is little mention of the why one ends up where they do. The basic tenements of the religion focus more on what we do while we are alive and how we worship than what happens in our afterlife. That said, reincarnation seems to be the most common fate for the deceased. Your deeds in life determined who or what you were reincarnation as in your next life. If you were good, you were reincarnation into a higher class. If you performed evil acts, you were reincarnated as a lesser class, or even as an animal or insect depending on severity. Later texts tell us that releasing our earthy ties, needs, and wants is the only way to break the cycle of reincarnation.

Buddhist traditions strive to break the cycle of reincarnation much the same as Hindu traditions. Many versions of Buddhist afterlife do not mention a judgement by a higher power, but an endless cycle of reincarnation on earth until a soul can reach Nirvana (paradise). Some traditions borrow Hindu thoughts on judgement and the cycle of reincarnation.

Here, we see the same common themes across all of these religions. The major difference between eastern and western religions seems to be reincarnation. Upon a closer look, the concept of reincarnation does not seem to be all that different from the western concept of hell, regardless of which religion you choose to compare it to. The notion that your past deeds determine your fate is prevalent throughout religion.

The descriptions above are simple, high level overviews of the various beliefs in the afterlife. I do not list them to change anyone's mind, or to convince you that one belief is better than the other. I merely list them to highlight the similarities in those beliefs and to give you an opportunity to review the beliefs for yourself.

Like many stories that are passed down from generation to generation, we risk losing key pieces of information. Bits of the story get changed here and there, much like when playing the game telephone. One person whispers in their neighbor's ear a phrase and that person whispers the same phrase in the next person's ear. By the time the phrase makes its way around the room, it is only a mere shadow of what it started about being. This is evidenced best in religion when we compare early Christian beliefs to our own modern beliefs.

Tiffany Ruiz, M.Msc.

Miguel

What I have found interesting in the past life regression sessions I perform with clients is that the vast majority of them describe a place with lights where they are surrounded by loved ones just before remembering their past life and immediately following recall of their death transition. No one yet has described this place as heaven, but what I have been told is that they felt it was more like a holding place. This is where their loved ones would make sure they were okay and they would receive a review of the life they lived. Very rarely, if at all, do my clients have to think about the lessons they needed to learn in that previous life. It is common for them to respond very quickly when they are asked "what lessons can you take from this life that can help you in this current one?"

Many times these realizations my clients have put their entire life into perspective for them. They begin to focus on things that are important, like family. They realize that the amount of time they have spent working and the material things they have been trying to attain mean very little and have actually been a distraction from what they needed to learn in this life.

One client in particular always comes to mind when I think about the life changing effects recalling a past life can have on ones' current life. Miguel came to me a complete skeptic. He did not believe 1) he could be hypnotized and 2) he certainly did not believe in having lived a life previously. What made him schedule an appointment remains a mystery and, truth be told, I was close to turning him away. I went forward with the session anyway because I felt this was important for him.

Miguel recalled a life in which he lost his entire family and was all alone. There had been a violent robbery and he the sole survivor. He felt incredibly guilty for being the remaining member of his family, as he was the leader he should have been the first one to die. He moved through many emotions as he recalled that life; happiness, joy, pain, and sorrow. He became very emotional at one point and I had to ask him to view the scene from an observer perspective.

He died alone, having taken his own life, and as he moved through the death transition in his recall I asked him to tell me what he was experiencing. He recounted darkness, and a sense of floating. He noted that he was no longer physical but he still had consciousness. Soon he saw beings of light moving toward him, he noted a feeling of deep unconditional love. When I asked him what lessons he was able to learn from that life that could help him in this one, he immediately told me that he had to relive those lessons in this life because he failed in his previous. It is this life that he needs to learn his lessons.

He told me that he had not been good to his family and put material gains above their well-being. As a result, he made a lot of people angry with him and those people sought to hurt him and his family. He realized later that his family had not died but left him because of his inability to put their well-being first. He had been too ashamed to find them and never looked for them. He failed to help his family, he put material gains above what really mattered, and he made a lot of enemies along the way.

During his life review he realized that he has been on the same path in this life, and he was being given an opportunity to learn the lessons again. He told me after the session was complete that he was failing miserably, he recently was divorced and his new girlfriend was about to leave him as well. He worked a lot and focused much of his time on various projects that he hoped would pay him back two fold in the long run. He realized that now was his opportunity to make things right. He immediately understood what he needed to do.

I heard from Miguel about 6 months after our session. He told me that things got really tough for him right after his past life recall with me. His girlfriend left him but thanks to the lessons he remembered he knew what he needed to do to win her back. He cut down on the number of projects he had going on, vowed to have time specifically for his children and worked tirelessly on proving to his girlfriend that he was a changed man.

He told me that prior to our meeting he was angry and could not understand why everyone could not see how hard he was working for them. He realized afterward that he was not working for them, but for himself. He was being completely selfish and once he changed the focus of his drive amazing things started to happen. He and his children formed a much stronger bond than they had ever had. Not only that, he is now engaged to his girlfriend and they are planning their wedding.

Most importantly, he told me, he has rekindled his relationship with God. He spent many nights thinking about our session and was able to recall additional details afterwards. He began to go back to church regularly, and it became a focal point in his life. He found his center and realized that there is more to life than material objects. He is now happy with his new life and his new purpose.

I still don't know what drew Miguel to come and see me if he did not believe in reincarnation. I am not sure he even knows. What I do believe however is that there is a deep sense of knowing within all of us that we will be judged for our actions after we pass from this world. I also believe that we spend much of our lives searching for why we are here and how we can make a difference in the lives of others. Miguel now believes he has lived before and will most likely live again. Even if he did not believe in reincarnation following our session, one cannot deny that it had a profound impact on his quality of life immediately following his recall.

Our own subconscious remembers, on some level, that we are not just of this world. We are part of a much greater being and at some point, for reasons unknown to us, we were separated from that being and we need to reconnect. The lessons we learn, our trials and tribulations, are failures and success in this life all lead us to one place: the afterlife. Where we go when we get there? That is completely up to us.

It has been said that we are not given a choice in what lessons we need to learn, but how we learn those lessons is completely within our control. This is the true meaning of free will. We may have obstacles and tough times but how we choose to respond to them determines the outcome.

What does Miguel's story and free will have to do with the afterlife and religion? It has everything to do with it. At the beginning of this chapter, I noted that all of religion has one commonality and that is what happens to us when we pass. We have reviewed some major religions and I have given you a high level overview of the beliefs of those religions. Miguel needed to understand that he was not living his life in a way that showed he had learned lessons from his previous life. Had he been unable to break this cycle, it is possible he would return again in his next life and repeat the lessons until he learned what he needed to. He chose, following recall, to change the behaviors that had been harming those he loved and as a result he is no longer full of pain and sorrow. He now understands that there may be hard times but how he chooses to react to them and the actions he chooses to take make all of the difference in his happiness.

Miguel's recall is in line with the descriptions of afterlife above. He was in a place where he reviewed the actions of his previous life. He immediately understood that this life he was living was indeed a "do-over" and he needed to experience similar trials, and make different choices, to break the cycle. Once he understood this, his entire life changed for the better. It really is as simple as that.

Soul and Consciousness

What exactly is a soul? The answer to that question depends on who you ask. Religion and science differ on the definition. Religion takes a spiritual approach while science provides us with a more clinical explanation. That is quickly changing however, as science delves more deeply into what consciousness is. It seems that science is ever closer to proving consciousness, and its relation to the soul, as something that can be quantified. Conversely, science has already proven there is a very tangible energy that powers the human body.

While science is edging closer to "proving" consciousness and what it means for humanity, religion and spirituality have already explored that frontier. We can look to early civilizations to help us understand the difference between sprit and soul. We can also look to religious texts such as the Christian bible, the Torah, and the Quran. What becomes apparent very quickly is that, much like stories of the afterlife, the idea that spirit and souls are two separate entities seems to be commonplace.

To review all the various traditions, myths, and religious texts that reference the difference between spirit and soul would be a book in and of itself. Rather than attempt to review all the similarities and differences here, what I will attempt to do is give you a basic understanding of each and how each is important to the afterlife.

Spirit

"Anyone who becomes seriously involved in the pursuit of science becomes convinced that there is a spirit manifest in the laws of the universe, a spirit vastly superior to that of man." **Albert Einstein**

There is in the universe a Universal Consciousness. Everything that ever was, and ever will be, is manifest from this source. Those who are more scientific in thinking will refer to it as the Big Bang. Those who are more spiritual may refer to it as a Higher Power. Yet still, those who are more religious will refer to this omnipotent presence as God. In the end, it does not matter what it is called. It is the Source of All.

This presence is the source of all energy, including the energy that is contained within your body. The energy that fuels you has been around since the beginning of time. It is one small piece of the original energy that created the vast and incomprehensible universe. It is ever expanding, ever learning and ever changing.

As Albert Einstein theorized, energy cannot be

destroyed. It can only change state. Atheists believe that when we die, we cease to exist. Not only is this spiritually incorrect, it is scientifically incorrect. Since we are made of energy, we cannot be destroyed…ever. Thank you, science.

To expand on this theory, none of what we see is completely solid, including ourselves. Yes, you read that right. If you had a powerful enough microscope, you would see that you can quite literally see right through yourself and all other seemingly solid matter. You would also see that the space you believe is empty is not. That means that you are 100% held together by energy, you literally are a being of light. You are connected to everything you see and even that which you do not see.

This energy we are made of is our Spirit. It is the piece of us that is returned to the Universe when we pass on to the "next world". Once our physical bodies shut down it begins the process of decomposition. The energy that once held the atoms together returns to its origin, and various other lifeforms begin the process of retuning the shell to the Earth.

Ancient Egyptians referred to the Spirit as the

KA. Many times, per The Book of the Dead, dying meant returning to KA. In the Christian bible, we are told in Ecclesiastes 12:7, "Then shall the dust return to the earth as it was: and the spirit shall return unto God who gave it." You will find a similar theme among most major religions; just you will find a similar theme when looking at life after death scenarios.

Gregg Braden, author of The Isaiah Effect and The God Code, has done extensive research into the DNA correlation between the human race and this Universal Consciousness. He maintains that coded within our DNA is a hidden language that can be decoded using biblical alphabets. The message deciphered from this biblical alphabet contains one universal message, regardless of whom you are or where you come from, is this: we are all connected.

Even though we possess a piece of the Universal Consciousness, it does not mean that we are the Universal Consciousness. Just as your hand is a *part* of you, but *not* you so your spirit is a part of God, but it is not God. In a nutshell, your spirit is simply your connection to God – the Universal Consciousness.

It may seem strange to think that the energy you are using to read this book is billions of years old, but think about it this way: energy cannot be created nor destroyed, it can only change forms. That means that any and all energy you contain has been around since the beginning of time. When discussing what happens to this energy when we die, the real question is not whether we cease to exist, but rather what becomes of this energy when our physical bodies stop working.

Soul

"Every book, every volume you see here, has a soul. The soul of the person who wrote it and of those who read it and lived and dreamed with it. Every time a book changes hands, every time someone runs his eyes down its pages, its spirit grows and strengthens." — **Carlos Ruiz Zafón, The Shadow of the Wind**

Many times the words spirit and soul are used interchangeably. What needs to be understood is that these pieces of us are two separate entities. Spirit, we have discussed, is energy which gives us life and is a part of the Universal Consciousness. The soul, however, is uniquely ours and is a culmination of all of our experiences past, present, and future.

Recent scientific discoveries have shown that the heart contains its own set of neural pathways, completely independent of the brain, called Sensory Neurites. The heart is not controlled by the brain; rather it is the other way around. Looks like there was some truth to the saying "my mind knows it is wrong, but my heart doesn't care". The heart wants what it wants.

The Ancient Egyptians referred to the heart as IB and believed that at conception we are created our hearts are formed with one drop of our mother's blood. This is the center of all thought, free-will, emotion, intellect, etc. per the Ancient Egyptians. The heart plays a large role in their afterlife beliefs. Upon death, the heart would be weighed against the feather of Ma'at. The heart could not be too heavy with too much sin, or too light having been frequently taken advantage of. If it did not balance with the feather, the soul would be cast into oblivion.

Just as your spirit is part of a larger spirit, your soul is also a part of your spirit. It is the part of the spirit that learns and grows and it retains the lessons you learn every day. Think of it as going to school. You don't know what you don't know, right? As you learn new things, those lessons get stored in your mind until you are ready to put them to use. For example, you didn't know when you were young that fire burned. Someone either told you, or you touched the fire. You now know to not touch fire, or anything that is "hot". You don't have to think about it. You just "know".

Your soul collects these lessons as well but because your soul never dies it has been collecting this information since the beginning of time. Every new body it inhabits creates a new opportunity to learn new things and use the lessons it has learned in the past. Remember, the soul doesn't know what it doesn't know so it collects knowledge as it evolves. The lessons it does know get stored for later use. Therefore, many of our past traumas are relevant, and sometimes disruptive, to the lives we are living now. We will get to that in a bit.

Let us go back to the Ancient Egyptians, because they have the most comprehensive descriptions of the differences between soul and spirit. They identified the soul as BA. It is often depicted in Egyptian writings as a bird with the human head. It would seek to be reunited with the KA, or Spirit, after the weighing of the heart ceremony.

The BA was said to be the personality of the living body and is what would make an individual unique. Some texts suggest the BA could eat, drink, and have sex. It was also believed by some that the BA was not just a "part" of an individual but the individual him/herself. This makes sense as the belief was that the BA was the embodiment of the individual's personality.

The Science

Now we know that the Spirit is a part of the Universal Consciousness and our Soul is a part of our Spirit. We also know that, upon death of the physical body, our Spirit and Soul seek to reunite and subsequently reunite with the Universal Consciousness. That all may still seem a bit "woo woo" for us more analytical types. After all, science can't possibly be able to substantiate any of this. Can it?

It has been recently discovered that Sensory Neurites act and behave independently of the brain. It is now believed that our likes and dislikes are centered not in our brains, but in our hearts. This sounds suspiciously like the Egyptian's belief of the spiritual heart. In fact, the Ancient Egyptians revered the heart so much that great care was taken to leave it in tact inside the body while all other organs were removed.

December 3rd, 1967 the first heart transplant was performed. Since then, there have been tremendous advances in the field of heart transplants. One of the interesting fields of study to emerge from the procedure is personality changes in the recipients.

As more procedures were performed, stories began to emerge about recipient's likes and dislikes changing drastically. There seemed to be something much more than a lifestyle change due to a major life event going on. Upon receiving hearts, recipients seemed to be taking on the lifestyle choices, feelings, and personalities of their donors.

These changes were attributed to cellular memory, meaning the cells themselves were storing the memories and not the brain. In one instance, a young man received a heart from an avid biker who was struck and killed by a car. When the recipient woke following the transplant, he told his mom everything was "copacetic". His mom was taken aback by this statement as it was not something he would normally say. They learned later after meeting the donor's wife that "copacetic" was a word they would use to indicate everything was okay following an argument. The morning of the accident, the couple had argued and the donor had not had a chance to make amends. All parties believe this was the heart's way of reaching out.

Following another transplant, a gentleman noticed changes in his food choices. When he met up with the family of his donor he asked the one question that had been weighing on his mind "Did the donor like burger rings?" It seemed that the recipient could not get enough of them. The family confirmed that indeed "burger rings" were the donor's favorite food.

What is more, in one study a group of nurses focused in on 10 patients who were heart transplant recipients. They sought to find 2-5 correlations between the recipients and the donors' likes and dislikes as they related to food, activity, sexual preference, etc. One of the subjects who received a heart from a man, who was shot in the face, reported having dreams of a bright flash and a loud noise that would wake him up in the middle of the night. He had not previous knowledge of how his donor passed.

The stories of personality changes became so commonplace that studies were done to determine their validity. The changes of preference and the possibility that the recipient could take on the personality of the donor, was confirmed: it was possible. Albeit by a small margin, but science confirmed it. Again, thank you science.

These stories seem to line up quite nicely with what we have been taught about both our heart and our souls. They especially coincide with the knowledge the Ancient Egyptians had about IB, or our spiritual hearts. What's more is that science is finally catching up with what religion has taught us and we are learning that those stories we heard in bible school are not so farfetched after all.

What about our spirit? Can science measure that as well? Quantum physics is becoming much more main stream with each new discovery. Many of these discoveries are now challenging the accepted knowledge many of us have of consciousness, the universe, and the laws that govern it.

So mainstream, in fact, that numerous Universities are offering courses on consciousness, reincarnation, and other scientific anomalies as part of degree programs. The US military spent 25 million dollars on remote viewing research from the 1960's to 1995. Einstein himself conceded that there was a force within the universe much more powerful and larger than any of us can ever imagine.

Dr. Bruce Greyson, leading researcher and professor at the University of Virginia, gave a talk in India where he discussed the idea of consciousness. He maintains that one of the challenges when holding onto the notion that consciousness needs a brain is the high intelligence and function found in those with little to no brain tissue. During his talk he speaks about those who function quite normally, socially and intelligently, despite having "virtually no brain at all".

A high school honors student accepted into Smith College underwent surgery following a car accident. Prior to surgery an x-ray of her head revealed she had no cerebral cortex, only a brain stem. The brain stem is responsible for our basic motor skills, but does not have the "connections" to perform higher level tasks such as reasoning, thinking, etc. For those tasks, you need a cerebral cortex. At least we thought we did.

Harvard researchers at the Massachusetts General Hospital conducted an 8 week study on the effects of mindfulness meditation on the brain. They discovered that with an average of 27 minutes a day spent in meditation, the areas of the brain related to stress, emotion, etc., were physically altered. These findings contradict the belief that meditation simply makes you "feel better" because you are relaxing. It makes you feel better because you are healing and changing the brain.

Princeton University is currently conducting a large scale study into Global Consciousness. The idea is that if enough people think the same thoughts, those thoughts can affect the outcome of various events. They seek to determine if consciousness is located within the brain, or if it is bigger than us as part of a mind/matter connection.

What the study has revealed is that your thoughts do have the ability to affect the outcome of events. It also has shown that if a bonded couple thought the same thoughts, the frequency of the intended outcome increased significantly. So, Princeton has proved two heads are better than one. What about the Global Consciousness? How did they measure that?

Random number generators were set up in various locations worldwide. These number generators flash a series of 1s and 0s at a frequency of about 50/50.

The number of ones vs. the number of zeros remains steady until a major world event takes place, the death of Princess Diana or terrorist attacks for example. What the study found was that 4 hours before the 9/11 attacks on the World Trade Center, the generator spiked, producing more of one number than the other and continued throughout the event.

Could that mean there was a collective intuition that something was terribly wrong and the world, as we knew it, would be changed forever? It is interesting to note the "intuition" was not just a result of humans broadcasting their knowledge of the event telepathically. It seems the spike occurred during natural disasters when there could not have possibly been any real understanding of what is about to occur unless we were told.

The question most people tend to ask when discussing consciousness is "what about the Alzheimer's or dementia patients?" If our consciousness is outside our brain, why then do these individuals have such a difficult time remembering events and people that are so very important to them.

Consider the young man who fell ill as a young

boy and remained in a coma for the next 12 years. He was conscious the entire time and while he did not have control of his body, his mind functioned perfectly. He recalls passing those 12 years by watching the sun's shadows move across the room or watching two insects race.

There is also the case of the man who was in an auto accident. He, too, was in a coma and very much aware of his surroundings for 23 years. Both of these individuals were trapped inside bodies that did not function and they had no way of communicating that they were aware. Could the same be said for the mentally disabled, could it be that they understand on a soul/consciousness level but they cannot make their bodies respond appropriately? I don't know, I am not a scientist or a doctor but it is an interesting possibility.

Frequently those with dementia will become very cognizant in the moments before death. They laugh, joke, and hold conversations. The family is ecstatic they have their family member back. Just as suddenly as they regained their awareness, they pass from this world. Dr. Grayson has the best theory I have heard. He says it is as if as the brain dies, it releases the consciousness from its grasp and for a few precious moments they can communicate clearly.

These interesting studies and reports only serve to solidify what we already know in our hearts....er...souls. We have all heard the stories when we were little, either in Sunday school, or in vacation bible school, or from grandparents. Some of us may not have heard them until we were well into adulthood. It does not matter where we heard it, or if we heard it at all. We know, on some level, there is a Universal Consciousness that we are a part of.

From the heart retaining memories of experiences and preferences, to the "mind" operating without a brain, to the collective consciousness's ability to change the outcome of events, these are not just fantasy tales. These are facts. Science has wandered into the realm of spirituality and proven it is real.

We feel with our "hearts" and think with our "minds". We feel with our souls and think with our consciousness. We have the power within us, now, to harness this knowledge and transcend any obstacle we face. We have the power to release any energy or belief we picked up in a past life and move forward in a positive direction in our current life.

Even the most diehard atheists believe this to be true on a soul level. Have you ever met an atheist who did not just love Star Wars? Seriously, instead of telling atheists to pray for humanity ask them to use the Force, they'll get it.

The knowledge we are one with the Universal Consciousness is ingrained within us, programmed if you will. Our souls learn and grow with each lifetime, picking up new lessons and sometimes carrying baggage from past lives. Our souls seek to reunite with our spirits upon death of the physical body and that union seeks always to be reunited with the Universal Consciousness we know as God.

More information regarding these studies can be found on my website. Please take some time to visit and review the material suggested. They all contain additional and more detailed information that I hope you will find interesting.

Why Reincarnate

My purpose is not to convince you of the validity or reality of reincarnation. My goal is to simply present the facts as I believe them to be true and allow you to make your own decisions. That being said, you would not be reading this book if you did not already believe in the possibility of reincarnation, right?

The studies and scientific experiments discussed in the last chapter give us a clinical explanation regarding our consciousness and how we are connected to the whole. You can apply these findings to the stories contained within many religious teachings and historical documents. When you are able to make the connection between what science is doing and what you have been taught, you will see they are basically two sides of the same coin.

Proving reincarnation, however, is much different than proving there is a God. Much of our power structures the world over are rooted in religion and the belief that we will go to hell if we do not act, think, talk a certain way. Proving reincarnation will turn much of our beliefs about the world upside down. But, that is not why we are here. We already believe, don't we?

Let's move on to the "why". It is a question we have been asking everyone since we could talk. "Why?"

There are many different theories about why we reincarnate. In the most basic sense, we reincarnate because it is a law of nature. We are energy and energy cannot be destroyed, it can only change forms. That is a great explanation for the spirit but, what about at a soul level? Why do we retain those memories? Are there lessons to be learned from remembering past lives? Why don't we remember those lives? Are we supposed to remember those lives?

There is a never-ending sea of questions surrounding reincarnation and there do not appear to be a lot of good answers out there as to why. Except for the Dali Lama, we know why he reincarnates. What about the rest of us? Why do our souls continue this cycle lifetime after lifetime?

Dying To Be Reborn

Karma is the most common reason we are given for reincarnation. The theory is that we return to settle karmic debt, but what does that mean exactly? Most people believe that means paying for something bad you have done in the past. The reality is that karma is a bit more complicated than that.

If you can, think of life as a maze and the end is reuniting with the Universe. Each attempt to successfully complete that maze is one life. When you follow one path and it doesn't work, you have to return to the beginning and start again. Each attempt leaves you with a lesson; don't turn right, turn left here, etc. Often times we keep making the same wrong turn over and over and do not get anywhere until we change our direction. Sometimes, we can make that shift in the middle of the maze but many times we have to start over.

The reason we reincarnate is not because we have trauma or karma, it is because we simply did not complete the maze. We did not find our path. Like a mouse trying to get their cheese in a maze, we are simply balls of energy looking for the path of least resistance. When we find it, when we successfully complete the maze, we will be done.

This is not to say karma isn't real. It's just a bit more complicated than simply doing something bad in a previous life and paying for it in this one. It's about learning and growth and not repeating the same mistakes. For every action, there is an equal and opposite reaction. This again, my friends, is science.

There are four basic laws of karma. Whether we like it or not, everything we do falls into one of these categories.

Law of Consequence – All conditions of a previous life can be reversed in your next life. This includes financial, personal, and professional conditions. If you were rich and powerful in a previous life, you are subject to being powerless and destitute in this life. Have no fear though, it is subject to reversal in your next life.

Law of Cause and Effect – For every action we take, there is a reaction. This is our opportunity to learn and grow with each lesson we are given. If we fail to learn that lesson, we have to go back to the beginning of the maze.

Law of Grace- Treat others as you would like to be treated. This Karmic Law is the Golden Rule. If you are kind and gentle to your neighbors it inspires them to be kind and gentle to others. If you are rude and obnoxious, those around you will pick up on that energy and be rude and obnoxious to others.

Law of Compensation – What you sow, so shall you reap. If you plant a seed and water and care for it, it will give you a beautiful plant. If you plant a seed but do not care for it, it will not grow. The same is true for every facet of our lives. We get out of life what we put into it.

We need not wait until our next life to reverse our Karma. We can reverse our Karma now, in this life, regardless of when we took the action that created the karma. Life is not about doom and gloom and we are not here to only correct past wrongs. You can reverse it!

Look, you have free will. You are 100% free to choose which actions you take in this life. You have been given the skills and knowledge to make decisions that will benefit you and those around you. That knowledge may have come from friends, or mentors, but you have the "know how" to be a good and decent human being that makes good decisions. You may not have had the greatest parents and you may not be in the best personal situation currently. But, at the end of the day, the actions you take are yours and yours alone.

I know you may be thinking, "but my boss hates me and I've been looking for another job but can't find one, I'm about to lose my house and then I'll be homeless, the bill collectors won't stop calling and I don't have money to pay them, I wrecked my car and don't have money to get it fixed…life isn't fair! Tell me again how I have free will?"

I'm glad you asked. The answer is quite simple. We are not given a choice in the lessons we must learn, but we are given a choice in what we learn from those lessons. That, my friends, is free will in a nutshell.

Instead of looking at all the negative in your life, take a moment and reflect on the positives. Think about what decisions you made to get you where you are and how you can make better choices going forward. What lessons can you learn from your current situation? What can you do differently in the future?

I know that this is a book about reincarnation and how our previous lives affect our current ones. If there is one thing I want you to take away from this book, it is this: our past lives can, and do, affect our present lives but sometimes we incur just as much karmic debt in our current lives. If we don't reverse course now we will pay for it later.

Tiffany Ruiz, M.Msc.

Why Don't We Remember?

That's a great question. If we are destined to repeat the cycle until we learn our lessons, one would think we would be able to remember what we already learned so we don't make the same mistakes right? Seems like a legit assumption.

Earlier in this book we discussed how science is making new and exciting discoveries almost daily in the area of consciousness and the brain. We are now learning that our consciousness may not reside solely in our brain, if it resides there at all. Scientists have discovered areas of the brain responsible for various functions, but they have not been able to determine how they take those electrical pulses and turn them into images, actions, memories, etc. Modern science believes that our brains take in information from the time we are born and that is all we need to function. It does not take into account how we process that information into feelings, thoughts, or habits that shape "who" we are.

How your brain works can be likened to your cell phone. You use your phone to receive and send messages. However, if you take your phone apart you will not find any evidence of those messages. The messages are sent to a certain "frequency" and your phone is just the device used to translate those messages into a format that is easily understood by you. If your phone is broken, the messages are still received but are not able to be deciphered. The phone does not act without input from either a sender or receiver. Your brain operates in the same way, sending electrical signals and pulses but not making any decisions or actions on its own.

Most of us were taught in science class that we only use 10% of our brain. If we delve into the meaning behind that statement, we see that what we were being taught is that we are only actively using 10% of our cognizance. This is because our consciousness acts only on what it knows based on input received from the superconscious and subconscious levels. To tap into that other 90%, we need to access our sub and super consciousness.

Our conscious only reacts based on information received and can only operate on limited memory, which is why you can't remember what you wore 6 Tuesdays ago at 3 PM without accessing the subconscious. The subconscious is responsible for your long-term memory and requires some thought to recall dates and incidents. It is also responsible for your auto response functions, like walking and breathing. Your super-conscious is responsible for all things spiritual like prayer, meditation, even dreaming.

The conscious mind is like computer memory, and each part of our consciousness has a different capacity for memory. Our conscious mind is like a USB drive, the subconscious mind is like a hard drive, and our super-conscious mind is like the "cloud." Each has a different path to access the information, and each part is equally necessary for healthy function.

Our consciousness, as previously discussed, can only operate based on limited information received from the sub-conscious and super-conscious. It's like a USB drive, only limited information can be stored and accessed there. It only plays back, and acts on, what it knows. Everything else is stored for future use, or on as "as-needed" basis.

Our Sub-conscious is our connection to the world

around us. From the time we are born, and some believe while we are still in the womb, we are taking in information from our surroundings. These experiences and learned behaviors are stored within our subconscious mind for future use. We access them when we breathe, when we walk, when we do math, when we recall memories listening to a song or smelling a scent.

We can think of our sub-conscious as a computer hard drive. Only you can store information there, and sometimes you install information that runs in the background. You may have information that you need to save but only access rarely so you choose to archive it. Only you can access that information though, because you are the only one who knows how to access it. It too, is a like a tape recorder only playing back memories for our consciousness to act on.

Our super-conscious mind is our connection to God, the Universe, whatever you choose to call your higher power. We access this part of our consciousness whenever we dream, pray, meditate, etc. This part of the mind is only accessed when one is deep in thought as it is a hyper-conscious state.

Tiffany Ruiz, M.Msc.

It is like Cloud storage. Anyone can store information there, and anyone can access the same information from anywhere at any time if they have the right passwords and the right connection. It's not necessarily stored on any hard drive, or physical device, it's just there in cyberspace until you access it by using the web.

Both our subconscious (our connection to the physical world) and our super-conscious (our connection to our Higher Power) are constantly taking in information and storing it. Our consciousness's ability is limited to a very small amount of input at a time and only reacts based on what is stored in the sub and super conscious mind, everything else runs in the background.

During a past life regression, or other type recall, we are simply opening up the archived files and reviewing them. The cool thing is that these files can be accessed at any time by all of us. They sometimes ae accessed in the form of Deja-vu or via dreams or even just a spontaneous memory.

Why do kids remember past lives easier than adults?

Children are more likely to remember their past lives than adults. In fact, many of the stories about reincarnation in the west and east alike stem from children stating they do not belong with their current family. They mention their "other mommy" or may indicate that their current family was "chosen" by them. They tell intricate and detailed stories about their previous lives.

Dr. Ian Stevenson and Dr. Carol Bowman are the leading experts in studying reincarnation stories of children. Both have conducted numerous regressions and heard countless stories from children claiming to have lived before. Many of their cases have been documented and verified, such as the cases of Shanti Devi, or James Leininger.

Dr. Stevenson focused much of his work in the East because reincarnation is more readily accepted by society and therefore much easier to locate families that are willing to discuss their children's past life memories. In the West, however, reincarnation is often a taboo subject for many families and the past life recall by children is often dismissed as child fantasy.

My own fascination with reincarnation began when I was five years old. I had vivid dreams of a life I had lived before this one. These dreams were so vivid and real that I woke up screaming multiple nights in a row. I was watching a beheading, not my own but that of someone I cared about very deeply. It was done with a guillotine outside of a large brown building with flags and horses. What stuck out most for me was the green rolling hills and the damp air. I can still "feel" the weather on my skin and the panic in my soul when I think back to that memory.

I was not able to explain to my mom what I was seeing so she had me draw a picture. I had no clue what a guillotine was at five, or that they were no longer used in executions. In elementary school I made a remark to my teacher that I had seen an execution with a guillotine and he matter-of-factly told me I made that up. He informed me that no executions with a guillotine had taken place in Germany, where I had come from.

There were other memories as well. I distinctly

remember visiting a circular room with a beautiful paining of angels and other heavenly beings on the ceiling. I can remember walking into the room holding my mom's hand and looking up. The memory has always stayed with me and I had always assumed it was the Sistine Chapel because of the paintings on the ceiling. My mom told me many times that we did visit many of the castles and churches in Europe but we never visited the Sistine Chapel or any place with paintings on the ceiling. None the less, I was persistent we had been there together.

I searched and searched the internet looking for this room I knew I had been in, not because thought this was a past life memory but because I truly believed I had been there in this life and I knew I wasn't crazy. I had just about stopped searching when, at 38, I saw a Dior J'Adore Commercial with Charlize Theron. I about screamed at my husband, "OMG! Look! That's IT! It's the room!"

The commercial showed the ceiling of the room I remembered. It was Versailles, in France. I had seen pictures of Versailles before but never that particular ceiling and that was the one I remembered looking at while holding my mom's hand. I was not crazy after all, but I knew in that moment my memory was not of this life but of a previous one. I had been in France, at Versailles, as a child in a previous life and guillotines were used in France.

I spent entire life up to that point thinking I was either crazy or made things up and my memories were not to be trusted. If parents in the west asked more probing questions, or at the very least were more open minded, we may produce more well-rounded adults who are able to separate previous trauma from their current lives. This, of course, is only my opinion.

Dying To Be Reborn

Do We Transmigrate to other species?

I do not know. There are conflicting schools of thought about whether we transmigrate when we reincarnate and it depends on whether you are "old school' or "new school". Traditional reincarnation beliefs say that you can reincarnate as a plant, animal, or mineral (yes, mineral). The modern approach to reincarnation is that you can only reincarnate as a human, and sometimes as an alien (yes, an alien).

Personally, I like science and things that make sense. I tend to subscribe to the older school of thought here only because it makes sense. Plants and animals are energy just like we are, and their energy cannot be destroyed when they die either. Plants and animals respond to our energy just as we respond to theirs. We are all the same energy, part of the Universe. It also seems to be a good response to one of the most common questions regarding reincarnation: "If reincarnation is real, why are there more people on the planet than there were 100,000 years ago?" After all, our numbers on this planet increased once we started mining forests for homes, fuel, and other things. It could be possible that as we harvested the forests, the energy of those plants came back in a human form.

Modern schools of thought believe that we can only reincarnate as the species we were in a previous life. Some of these theories go a step further and insist that we also tend to reincarnate in the country we died in. I am not sure how the soul honors borders, but that is the theory. Those who believe this theory also tend to believe that we may have lived our previous lives on another planet and have chosen to reincarnate here. This is their answer to the population increase, and it also seems to be validated by the number of western regressionists whose clients have recalled lives as beings from other planets.

Many of the great philosophers to include Pythagoras, Plato, and Aristotle believed plants had souls themselves. Some even believed we incarnated as plants and animals. Such was the case with Empedocles who believed he was not only reincarnated from a bird and fish, but once as a bush. There is nothing that makes me stop and think this is so farfetched that it is not possible. As I have said, I tend to agree with this theory but I must admit I have not had any clients recall life as a fern and I don't know any other regressionists whose clients have either.

This must be one of the unanswered questions for now. I encourage you, as always, to take what you learn and do more research. After you have done that, form your own opinion. I look forward to your own theory!

Tiffany Ruiz, M.Msc.

How can I remember my own past life?

There are many ways we can recall previous incarnations. One of the most commonly known today is by using hypnosis using what is referred to as regression therapy. Other methods include spontaneous recall, dreaming, déjà vu, and meditation.

Spontaneous recall can happen when you are watching a movie, visiting a place you have never visited before, or while simply performing a mundane task while washing dishes. Those who experience spontaneous recall describe it as being similar to a feeling of déjà vu but recall an actual event being played out. This recall typically happens when a person is focused and in a "zone", or self-hypnotic or meditative state when the mind can access the its archives.

Dreams are another way to recall your previous lives and can also happen spontaneously. Many of my clients report having dreams that have expanded on their past life regressions following a session with me. This happens because when we sleep, we are more open to accessing those memories. Some assert that dreaming is the way our minds sort through the various challenges we face in our waking moments to come up with solutions. I believe that accessing our mind's past life archives is just one way our mind searches for answers.

Déjà vu is the feeling or sensation of having experienced something before. Many people attribute it to a past life experience but I do not believe that is entirely the case. I have had many clients experience a sensation like déjà vu when visiting a place that seems familiar but they have never visited. It is those experiences I feel are indications of having lived a life previously. The déjà vu many of us experience, the feeling we have had a conversation before or been in a particular situation already, are "check-in" points to let us know we are on the right track and we are following our plan as laid out in our life between life reviews.

Past life regressions and guided meditations are the most common way people recall their previous lives today. This can be accomplished with either an experienced and qualified hypnotist who facilitates the session, a pre-recorded self-hypnosis session, or by meditating on their own.

As a past life regressionist I see many clients who simply want to "know" who they were in a past life. The vast majority of my clients however feel they have some lingering trauma from a previous life that they would like to resolve. They may have an unexplained phobia, or they have been to a Dr. for a recurring physical symptom for which the Dr. cannot give a diagnosis other than "stress".

When clients visit me for a past life regression, I do not care whether they fully believe in reincarnation or not. The experience, in my opinion, speaks for itself. There are reports upon reports of mysterious pain and unexplained phobias resolving themselves following a past life regression, whether the client believes or not. It seems once the brain makes an association with a particular ailment and a memory or scenario, it seems to say "oh, I know what it hurts now, never mind, let's move onto something else".

All of that said, always visit your doctor first. Always. Pain is the mind's way of notifying us of something wrong, either physiologically or mentally. Every cause that can be ruled out must be ruled out prior to turning to past life regression. I have said it before, and I will say it a million times, not everything that happens to us in this life is the result of a previous life.

Even pains and discomforts that seem to have no cause are not necessarily the result of a past life trauma. A pain in the neck or back, for example, can be attributed to events that are happening to an individual in real time. Remember, pain is the mind's way of telling you something is wrong. If someone is being what you describe "a pain in the neck" that is exactly where that unresolved stress may manifest itself.

Past Life Regression, to resolve these phobias and pains, should only be used when all other causes have been ruled out. When no other root cause can be identified, PLR is an excellent resource for an individual to explore. Many who have used this method have reported immediate relief from various ailments that their medical practitioners had not been able to relieve with traditional methods.

So now that we have a basic understanding of how reincarnation is possible, why remembering past lives may be good for you, and how it can help you, the only question left is: what exactly can YOU use past life

Tiffany Ruiz, M.Msc.

regressions for?

Lessons and Resolutions

Connecting with Soul Groups

"But, he/she is my soul mate!" We all have that one friend, don't we? They seem to find their soul mate every other week. The love affair is strong, they seem to have known each other forever, and they forsake everything else for this one person. And then, just as quickly as it began, it's over. Just like that.

Is this just wishful thinking, or could these individuals really be their soulmates? It is completely possible that these individuals are soul mates and were meant to meet for a brief period in this life. It could be that the lessons both individuals needed to learn could be resolved in a short period or it could be that one individual's lesson is that of a "revolving" door of lovers.

The common misconception about soul mates is

that we are to find them and spend the rest of their days with them. The problem with believing this theory is that some people spend their whole life searching for their "other half" and completely miss the meaning of those relationships that are the most impactful for them and their journey.

Soul mates are those souls who we are meant to meet in this life but they are not necessarily a romantic partner. They are meant to help us learn lessons, to move forward in our maze of life. These relationships may be comfortable relationships like those we have with friends and family. They can also be difficult, like those we have with people we do not like or those we have frequent run-ins with.

This is not to say that we do not have a soul mate that we are meant to spend the rest of our lives with. For some of us, that may be the case. However, what happens more frequently is our reincarnation with what are known as soul groups. These are groups of souls that reincarnate together in a particular lifetime and whose lessons to be learned are intertwined in some way.

During our life review and preparation for this

life, we review the lessons we need to master in order to move forward. During this time, other souls are a part of our plan, and we are a part of theirs. Despite what many popular theories would have you believe; these relationships are not always all good and full of love and happiness. Sometimes these relationships are tough, and painful. These tough relationships however are instrumental to our learning and should not be dismissed as chance encounters.

Many times, our soul groups incarnate together over many lifetimes, changing roles. Someone who was your mother in a previous life may return as a spouse in this one. A child in a previous life may return as a friend or a boss in this life. A slave owner in a previous life may return as a parent in this life.

While these roles may be changed over different lifetimes, the lessons that need to be learned don't necessarily change. For example, a slave owner in a previous life may return as your overbearing and overprotective mother in this life. Your lesson may be to learn to break free of the perception that someone else controls you, to learn how to interact with that individual and still maintain your own sanity and build your own life.

A jealous co-worker who seems to undermine your every move may have once been a step-child who was jealous of your relationship with their parent in a previous life. Perhaps your lesson is not that you must learn how to deal with jealous people but that you need to understand their struggles and maybe see things from their perspective. Or, maybe you need to just learn to be tolerant and extend compassion and understanding. Then again, it could be your lesson is simply to learn how to break ties with this individual who has brought you so much frustration, rather than trying to continue to make amends.

There is a theory that, during our life review, we create contracts with these soul mates prior to incarnation. This may be the case; I have many clients who have reported recalling making these contracts during their regressions. The most interesting thing for me is that all my clients who report recalling this process describe very similar experiences. Their soul groups appear as "specks" or "points" of light, there is more of a "knowing" than a speaking interaction, and there is always some form of negotiation in the form of "I agree to do this but not that".

In negotiation, our soul mates agree to behave or act in a certain way to play out the lessons we need to navigate in our incarnations. Because in the most basic form, our souls understand that we are only energy looking for the path of least resistance, they are sometimes hesitant to create any sort of friction that will impede that path. Thus, the negotiation process begins. A soul may agree to create an obstacle to you overcoming a fear but will not make that obstacle something that could harm you physically.

The most important thing to remember when attempting to connect with soul groups, or searching for your soul mate, is to remember to let go and let your pre-designed plan play out. Every interaction we have and every significant relationship is a lesson to be learned. Once again, we are not given a choice in the lessons we get to learn but we are given a choice in how we learn those lessons.

Tiffany Ruiz, M.Msc.

Behaviors

If a soul left a previous incarnation unexpectedly, was not ready, or by way of a traumatic death that individual may display behaviors that are reminiscent of that life. These behaviors may manifest in any variety of ways from a fear or phobia to depression. The key indicator, after all medical avenues have been explored, is that there does not seem to be any root cause for the behavior.

PTSD or, Post Traumatic Stress Disorder, is a mental disorder which is characterized by having witnessed a terrifying or horrific event and failing to recover. The sufferer is triggered by events that bear a resemblance to that event and begin to relive it in their mind. Most recently soldiers returning from war have been in the spotlight as being the most likely to suffer from PTSD. They are not the only group affected however, rape victims, accident victims, etc., also suffer and relive their traumas when triggered.

While there are specific criteria that one needs to meet to be diagnosed with PTSD, at its very core is a very real fear of the individual having to relive a terrible or horrifying experience. During Fourth of July celebrations, for example, those who have recently returned from a war zone may associate the loud booms of fireworks with bombs detonating. They are likely to experience a flash-back of the experience and be instantly transported mentally to that time, complete with all of the fear and anxiety it brings.

Our souls are not so different. After our life reviews, we return as our new incarnations. We have not fully forgotten our previous lives, however. Just as we associate fears and physical symptoms with traumatic experiences in this life, our souls also experience these "flash-backs" when presented with various experiences in this current incarnation. The physical symptoms and behaviors are manifest in this life, but are a direct result of traumatic experiences from a previous life.

These symptoms can present themselves in a variety of ways, from emotional to physical. The following are just a few of the ways people have experienced these symptoms. These ae not the end-all be-all however and the best way to find out how your past life is affecting you in this life is to visit a qualified Past

Tiffany Ruiz, M.Msc.

Life Regressionist.

Identity

There are many people who do not identify with their current bodies, they feel out of place and see a stranger when looking in the mirror. This feeling of being born in the wrong body is so strong that it affects every aspect of the individual's life and they may become depressed. The most common example are Transgendered individuals, but there are also those who identify as disabled when they are not, or as a different race than what they were born as.

Eating Disorders

An individual who suffered rejection in a previous life may feel the need to waste away and become as small as possible so they do not have to suffer the same rejection in this life. This may manifest itself as anorexia or bulimia. On the other hand, obesity may stem from severe malnutrition in a previous life resulting in an obsession with food so the soul never has to experience that again.

Addictions

As with obesity, individuals who overuse sex, shopping, money, fast cars, etc., may be attempting to avoid the pain of deprivation they experienced in a previous life. They may need to secure their status and ensure they have enough this time around. Those who overuse alcohol or drugs may be attempting to escape the reality in this life so as not to relive the pain of the previous.

Depression

There are many people who suffer from depression with no identifiable cause. Medications do not seem to help alleviate their feelings of melancholy. It is possible that these individuals have carried over feelings of a traumatic loss or a great upheaval from a previous life that is manifesting as depression in this life.

Anxiety

Anxiety can manifest from a past life experience of being wronged, have something taken from you unfairly, losing something very important to you or simply not knowing what happened not having this resolved in a previous life.

Insecurity

Someone who was abandoned in a previous life may have an unexplainable need to be loved and accepted in this life. This feeling of needing to be needed usually manifests in individuals who seek out abusive relationships or who have a series of relationships in which they themselves become obsessive over their partner out of a fear of rejection.

Fears and Phobias

It is important to note that fears are a natural response to danger and instrumental to our survival. Phobias, on the other hand, is an irrational fear. For example, being afraid of sharks is natural. Being afraid of sharks to the point of not being able to get in and enjoy the ocean is a phobia. It is a debilitating fear of something that does not pose an immediate threat. Personally, I am so afraid of sharks that I cannot even be near a small one in a fish tank without my heart racing.

These phobias can stem from a traumatic death in a previous life when the cause of death was directly related to what the individual is afraid of in this life. These phobias commonly manifest from drowning,

Dying To Be Reborn

burning, suffocating, falling, etc.

Body Syndromes

The body/mind connection is very strong and when we think or say certain phrases the body can interpret them quite literally. As an example, thinking someone is a "Pain in the neck" can result in an actual pain in the neck. Many of these physical symptoms may have started as a past life experience, either from actual traumas or as a reaction to an experience. Remember, the conscious mind does not make decisions, it only makes associations based on experiences of the subconscious mind.

Headaches / Migraines

This can indicate some injury in a past life, or an inability or refusal to make a decision. In other words, not using your head.

Eyes

Issues with eyes can signal having witnessed a horrific event and are now blinding oneself from any future similar events.

Skin

Recurring skin problems can indicate a need to crawl out of ones' skin due to being uncomfortable in a situation or a result of deep rooted emotions that are "boiling to the surface". It can also indicate a severe skin trauma in a previous life such as being burned.

Stomach

Unresolved anger, fear, or important things left unsaid can be responsible for digestive issues in this life.

Shoulders

Pain or other issues in these areas could be the result of carrying heavy burdens in a previous life.

These are just a few examples of the ways our subconscious manifests our struggles physically. It is important to remember that we should not assume these body syndromes are a direct result of a past life. Body syndromes can manifest at any point in our lives.

Recently, my husband and I had some heated arguments. I was very angry with him, with myself, and even contemplated divorce for a brief second. A couple days later, my ring finger started itching terribly. I took my ring off and noticed that the skin beneath my wedding ring was raw, red, and irritated. Now, I have worn this ring for 21 years and have never had this happen. This was my body's way of manifesting my feelings during that brief time. Of course, I don't really want a divorce, but in that moment, my anger manifested physically.

I have zero doubt my husband and I have been together through many lifetimes and have switched roles a few times. I don't feel that every physical symptom I have is related to this long-term love affair. Sometimes, we just simply give each other headaches and that is all they are. We do however share the same birth marks and I do believe those are related to our previous lives.

Birth Marks / Birth Defects

Dr. Ian Stevenson researched the correlation between birthmarks and past lives extensively. He compared many autopsy photos to the birthmarks of his subjects. He studied the trajectory of bullets to the birthmarks and found matches. He also compared the memory of his subjects past lives to the autopsy reports and the stories of those associated with the subject's past life. It is quite an interesting research study and more information can be found in his book, Twenty Cases Suggestive of Reincarnation.

Many skeptics dismiss the idea of any correlation between past life trauma and birthmarks because, on the surface, it just does not make sense. If we take a step back and remember that our bodies are only energy that form from manifested thoughts, then we begin to see how these birthmarks are indeed possible.

If our physical bodies were harmed during a previous life, the soul (or our energy) may remember that injury and manifest it while forming into the new body. If, in a previous life, you were a soldier who had a limb amputated then you may return with either a missing limb or partial limb. Of course, there is no guarantee that your limb will be missing or abnormal in your next incarnation, but there does seem to be evidence supporting this claim according to Ian Stevenson.

There are enough books and YouTube videos showing how birthmarks and disfigurements can correlate with a traumatic death in a past life so I will not waste your time regurgitating those here. If you are interested in those stories, I strongly encourage you to get your hands on a copy of Dr. Ian Stevenson's Twenty Cases Suggestive of Reincarnation.

Most of us have birthmarks on our bodies, but can they all be from a previous life? Some I believe are simply marks we have from when our bodies are developing. Most however, I believe are our soul's way of remembering the way the body "was" and it redevelops that way. Again, and I cannot stress this enough, our spirits and souls are energy and energy is consciousness and it is able to learn and grow. Our bodies are only a vessel to hold the spirit and soul. If you had a shiny new car and it was dented, when you get it repaired the damage is still there but it was fixed. The same is true of our bodies, the dents and dings have been repaired but we can see where it was repaired.

I have numerous marks on my own body. Some are just beauty marks and others are, I believe, the result of a previous life. Most notably, a raised bump between my eyes, a mole on the middle finger of my right hand, five birthmarks on and around the armpit of my right arm, and what appears to be a shotgun wound on my lower right abdomen with an "exit wound" mole on my back.

My husband and youngest son both have corresponding marks on their right hand middle finger. My husband has the same marks under his right arm as I have on my right arm, they are nearly identical. I have not regressed to those lives where those marks come from yet, but do know we have shared the same experiences in previous lives.

It is important to note that I have not told my family, or anyone, about many of the regressions and memories I have had personally because I want to see if they have the same or similar memories as I have. If I told them what my memories are, then I am afraid I will taint the regression and I want it be as truthful as possible.

Make no mistake I believe in reincarnation, but I still want to test the soul group theory. That is the researcher in me.

My youngest son allowed me to do a regression with him. He recalled getting off a train in the late 1800's and looking around for someone. The town was dusty and the only thing around was the train station. He recalled people walking back and forth while he stood there looking for someone. That someone never showed up to meet him and he felt abandoned and alone.

What he did not know then is that during one of my own regressions, I too had a memory of stepping of a train at a dusty train station sometime in the late 1800's. I can recall the pale blue of my dress, my feet feeling very uncomfortable in my shoes, and looking down at my hands. Current me had a thought as soon as I looked down at my hands, "these are my hands, but they can't be". I recalled the name Tilly and had the strangest feeling that I was supposed to meet someone there but they never showed up.

I believe this was a life we shared but we missed each other at the train station. I don't believe we ever reconnected during that life but we are together now and I am his mom. He told me after his regression that he no longer feels alone, as he had before. He felt that we simply missed each other at the train station that day and were unable to find each other again.

The name Tilly sparked my curiosity and I began researching the name, the time period, and train stations in dusty towns. I happen to live in what is still a dusty town. Okay, it is a sprawling city now but it is still dusty. Out in the West Texas Town of El Paso lived a very successful Madam named Tilly Howard. Photos of her establishment show fine furniture and draperies, nothing but the best European flare. I thought the pieces fit, as I do adore 1800 Victorian furniture and have always been a strong and independent woman. The town, the name, and the time period seemed to fit but my soul did not resonate. My thoughts always drifted back to my gunshot birthmark on my lower abdomen.

I had always had abdominal problems the Dr. could not diagnose. Sharp stabbing pain in my abdomen would have me doubled over in agony. The pain was always located in the lower right side of my abdomen where my birthmark is. Once, the doctor diagnosed it as early menstruation cramps when I was young but, mostly it was diagnosed as stress. It was not until a surgery I had removed much of the "splatter" dots did the pain go away permanently. I still have a few dots and a large circular spot but the majority of the splatter is gone.

This mark, that I intuitively knew as a gun shot wound, is the one my mind kept returning to when I thought about Tilly Howard. The pieces fit but it didn't seem right. Until, one night, I had a dream of arguing with a lady. We were dressed appropriately for the late 1800's and I was accusing her of taking something that belonged to me. I became enraged and hit her. She then shot me in my lower abdomen at close range. That is where my dream ended, but I could not stop thinking about Tilly Howard and what that had to do with my birthmark.

One night, while researching Tilly Howard, I came across a story about the El Paso Brothels and lo and behold there was a story about two El Paso Madams who had an altercation. Etta Clark had coerced one of Fat Alice Abbot's ladies into working for her. When Alice found out, she went over to Etta Clark's and demanded her girl be returned. The argument turned violent and

Dying To Be Reborn

Etta shot Alice with a .44 revolver, right in the pubic arch.

The papers reported it as the "Public Arch" and Fat Alice, who was 300 lbs. and 6' tall, was incensed and offended. She threated the editor of the paper who quickly skipped town. If she was truly shot in the pubic arch, and I am indeed the reincarnation of Fat Alice, then that is where my birthmark should be. However, my mark is slightly to the right of pubic arch. Could the editor have taken liberties with the story and reported it as not the pubic arch, but the "Public Arch" for sensationalism? Is that why Alice was so enraged? I believe so.

Am I the reincarnation of Alice Abbot? I cannot say for sure. If that is the case, why didn't I receive the name Alice, but instead got "Tilly" when I regressed? I learned later that Alice sold her brothel, along with the furniture and draperies, to Tilly Howard when she retired. This would account for why I remembered the name Tilly. One thing is for certain, I identify more with Fat Alice, than I do the young and beautiful Tilly Howard.

There is much more to the story, but I am

reserving the rest for another time. I would like to see if anyone else in my close circle of friends and family has memories of this time before I divulge the rest. I believe at least two people in my soul group have ties to that period and I do not want to taint their memories beyond what I have said here.

One thing is certain, if the shooting was not traumatic enough for Fat Alice, that trauma was compounded by how the story was reported. The trauma and embarrassment this incident would have caused someone would be enough for the birthmark to resurface even if it was not the cause of death. The soul, while forming the body in the womb, would remember the scar of that trauma and that area could possibly have developed in the shape of the wound.

I believe that the soul remembers all trauma, not just trauma that results in death. However, for the trauma to manifest across incarnations it must be serious enough to cause mental anguish. The pain of the trauma must be so great that it creates PTSD like symptoms in the soul for it to manifest physically in a person's subsequent lifetimes.

Your Own Past Life Recall

My any hypnotherapists complain that stage hypnotists give the profession a bad name and a false impression of what hypnosis is. I believe the same is true with many regressionists who publish stories of "proven" reincarnation. There is always a pre-conceived notion when clients come to see me that they will remember everything in high definition detail, from people and places to times and dates. They seem to think that because they watched a YouTube video of "10 Cases of Reincarnation That Will Astound You", their memories will be just as vivid and if not, then it is not real. Like that commercial said, that's not how this works. It's not how any of this works.

Children seem to remember their previous lives vividly and have difficulty in separating a previous life from this one. As we begin to store memories and experiences in our current incarnation, memories from our most recent life become archived. We begin to acclimate to our current incarnation and let go of any lingering ties to the past.

If we think back to what religions have taught us, we remember that we passed through the waters of forgetfulness. We are not meant to remember those lives. We need to move forward, and continue our journey. We cannot, and will not, make progress if we are stuck in the past.

Alright, I know what you are thinking. How can I, a past life regressionist, who helps people remember their previous lives, say that we are not supposed to remember a past life? I understand how that can be seen as contradictory. I can assure you it is not. As with anything, there are always exceptions to the rule. The one-offs, if you will.

In its most basic form, our souls today are the exact same souls from thousands of years ago. The experiences we had serve to teach our souls and help us navigate toward our ultimate goal. In other words, we are meant to remember what we have learned from our lessons but not necessarily the lessons themselves.

Remember, our consciousness does not make decisions, it makes associations, so when we are faced with a similar trauma the soul reacts in the only way it know how because that is what it has learned.

We need not remember the actual circumstances of an event to experience the feelings it gave us. Smelling a perfume your mother wore may trigger feelings of love and safety. Hearing a song you listened to with a former lover may trigger deep emotions such as nostalgia or even sadness. This is no different than "triggering" a memory of a previous life by visiting a place frequented in a previous life, or coming into contact with a member of your soul group unexpectedly.

Even though the doors on the past are closed, it does not mean we cannot or should not open them. In this life, if we have a need to visit a therapist to heal, that process typically involves revisiting the incident by discussing it and working through various ways of understanding the root cause of the problem. We do the exact same thing when working through past life issues, we revisit the incident.

Our memories, however, whether from this life or

a previous one, are not always 100% accurate. In recent survey published in the PLoS Journal on Aug. 3, 2011, it found that almost 2/3 of Americans believe our minds record memory like a video camera and everything we do is recorded exactly as it happened.

On the contrary, researchers from the same survey noted only a 30% accuracy rate among even the most confident of eyewitnesses. That means that 70% of people incorrectly remember events, and cannot be depended upon should they need to testify in a criminal trial.

55% of respondents felt that hypnosis is useful in jogging memory. However, memory recalled under hypnosis is only as accurate as a regular memory with a 30% accuracy rate. Moreover, when someone is in a state of hypnosis, they are 200x more suggestible. This means that a hypnotist can "lead" the memory and, in an effort to please the hypnotist, the subject can create memories. It is for this reason that memories recalled under hypnosis are not admissible in a court of law.

When I assist a client with a past life regression, I try not to lead my clients. It is not always that easy to do.

I see many regressionists suggest asking a client to describe their shoes. By asking a client to describe their clothes or shoes, we are making an assumption that there are clothes or shoes to be described. Something as simple as "what is on your feet" puts a suggestion in the client's mind that there must be feet. But, what if the client was an amputee in that life? We have just created a false memory.

Remember when I mentioned I did not want to divulge any more about my own past life memories because I did not want to taint the memories of others? This is the reason. If I say I believe someone was present during one of my memories, then I am planting the expectation in their mind. This is also why I am so confident in the past life memory my youngest son had. I never told him about the train station, or described it to anyone before he had the recall. That short snippet in time and his recollection of the buildings and his description of the scene is enough to convince me. There was no elaborate story that went along with it, it truly was only a snippet.

This is the way most past life recalls go, snippets of a time past. Glimpses, flashes, fleeting images or emotions or thoughts and then, a knowing. It is sort of like someone saying "first grade" and you have a flash in your mind's eye of your first grade school picture. Then, you just know that first grade means learning to read and sitting in a desk and story time. You just know, you might not remember every single thing that happened in first grade but you have an idea.

You remember friends' names, you remember your first grade teachers name, you remember where you went to school. You might recall playing at recess, or lunch time in the cafeteria. That might lead to remembering a fight you had with your best friend and how much your feelings were hurt. That makes you remember your pet goldfish who died and how sad that made you feel. All of these memories come flooding back and none of them play fully in your minds eye, you just remember how it happened.

Just as our recalled memories in this current incarnation are fractional, so are the memories of our previous life. No two people remember events in exactly the same way, either. To top it off, memories are not always remembered like movies. They can be felt, or heard, or even smelled. Because of this, I simply cannot subscribe to the recalls that describe in vivid detail conversations, places or events, etc. I can, however, believe in the overall recollection of those events.

I have little doubt there were recalls, and I fully believe in the work that my fellow regressionists do. However, as I tell my own clients, I want you to be fully informed about what you may experience and I sure do not want you to be disappointed when it does not go as you imagined.

You can experience the regression in any number of ways. There is absolutely no right or wrong way to recall a memory. Whether that memory is from this life or not, you will experience the memory exactly in the way that is right for you.

Tiffany Ruiz, M.Msc.

The Restaurant

When I first started doing regressions I had a client who was very excited about the prospect of having a PLR session. I did a standard breakdown of what hypnosis is, explained how regressions can help one overcome fears and past trauma. This client, however, only wanted to experience who she was in a time past.

I did a standard regression but she was not able to visualize anything. I asked her to tell me what a pine tree looks like, and she could describe it but maintained she still could not visualize it. I continued with the session, taking her to a previous life. I asked her to describe where she was, to say the first thing that came to mind.

She was quickly becoming frustrated with the session and she brought herself out of hypnosis. After some discussion, she agreed to try again. This time I asked her to describe what she was feeling and not what she was seeing.

She stated she thought she was in room. She had a flash of a fancy set table. She continued to state she could not "see" anything. Her inability to visualize was too much and she brought herself up out of hypnosis again.

While we were chatting about the experience, she sniffed the air. Yup. She sniffed the air and asked me if I smelled steak. "I am starving", she said. And then, she got this look of knowing across her face and exclaimed "I was in a restaurant! I was eating steak!"

She only had one session and moved to Paris the following week. A "psychic" had told her about her past life and she wanted to be able to experience it for herself. It was not what she expected and I suspect she was very disappointed in the experience. As far as I know, she was never able to fully delve into that other time.

I make it a point now to really review the process with my clients and make sure they understand that they may not actually visualize a scene. It may be a memory, or a knowing, or they may smell something, they may even hear something. I cannot say what they will see, or how they will experience their memories. This is their journey, and their path. I am only the guide.

Tiffany Ruiz, M.Msc.

Why Reincarnation Matters

What does all of this mean for us? How does this knowledge and newfound understanding help us in our current life? Does it even matter if we believe in reincarnation, or not? If we are unable to answer these questions, then this book has been a waste of time.

We started this journey with a discussion about the afterlife and how various religions have shaped our understanding of what that may look like. We touched on the similarities each religion shares when it comes to death. We learned the importance death plays in religion.

We also discussed the difference between the spirt and soul. We touched on consciousness and whether it originates in our brains, our hearts, or none of the above. We looked at the ways recalling past can resolve various traumas.

What we did not discuss is why reincarnation is important as a religious belief. Most importantly, we did not review how we can use reincarnation to get closer to God, or our Higher Power.

Before Ian Stevenson, Dr. Brian Weiss, and other scientists and regressionists, reincarnation was a long held religious belief. It continues to be one of the basic tenants of Eastern religions today. Sadly, the same is not true in the West.

The last 50 years have seen an ever increasing interest in reincarnation and the possibility of past lives. Stories like Bridey Murphey, James Lininger, and others have brought reincarnation home and made it real. We have had many respected doctors and medical professionals do studies and write books on the subject. And yet, even with all of the stories and studies, reincarnation is still a fringe belief.

It seems to get lumped in with ideas of ghosts, big foot, and aliens. Not to take away any validity those topics may possess, but reincarnation is a religious belief. In case I was not clear here, reincarnation is a religious belief.

Yes, it is 100% spiritual, and you do not have to be religious to believe in reincarnation. However, reincarnation was, and is, the very foundation for many religions to include Christianity and other Abrahamic religions.

Numerous references can be found regarding reincarnation in ancient texts, including the bible. It was, and is, a very important part of Christianity and we have forgotten it.

We did not forget by happenstance, either. In the 6th century A.D. the Byzantine Emperor Justinian along with his wife, Theodora, conspired with the church to remove all traces of reincarnation from religious texts and doctrine. As a result, for the next 1,400 years, until present day, the Christian Church has considered reincarnation blasphemous. The statement issued by the 5th Ecumenical Council of 553 AD was, "Whosoever teaches the doctrine of a supposed pre-birth existence of the soul, and speaks of a monstrous restoration of this, is cursed."

This ban did not happen until 600 years following Jesus's death. Until then, reincarnation was a foundation of the Church and of Christ's teachings. Some references can still be found in the bible today and the bible as a whole becomes clearer and more meaningful if we approach it with knowledge of reincarnation.

Reincarnation is the evolution of the soul. Each earthly lifetime is an opportunity to grow spiritually and get closer to God. Every action we take in this life is an opportunity to understand the bigger picture.

If we can accept that we are all but one piece of the greater consciousness, then we can truly start to move forward and make our way through this maze of life. We have never truly died, and we never will. We will continue to live on, to grow and navigate our way back to God.

If there is one thing I want you to take away from this, it is this: reincarnation is not a birth and rebirth cycle. It is the journey of your soul and its navigation back to the Universal Consciousness. Each lifetime is simply changing the vehicle in which we navigate that journey.

Your purpose is not to understand that true power is outside of you in the form of riches, or power, or even religion. Your purpose is to understand that true power is within you, that you are a divine being capable of great things because you possess the power of the Holy Spirit. As Jesus said, the Kingdom of Heaven is within you.

Once you have truly embraced this knowledge, you will have finished the maze and can return both Spirit and Soul to the Greater Consciousness. In the meantime, we will continue to get a new vehicle in the form of a new body every few years.

Whatever you have to say about reincarnation, just don't call it a comeback. We've been here for years.

ABOUT THE AUTHOR

Rev. Tiffany Ruiz, M.Msc. is past life regressionist and hypnotist. She provides a soul-centered approach to helping others achieve their goals and overcome self-imposed obstacles through hypnosis.

Tiffany offers online and in-person past life regressions and spiritual counseling that allows her clients to access their True Self and release all negative thought processes that may be holding them back from achieving their goals.

She resides in El Paso, TX with her husband and their 4 dogs and 1 cat. She has three children who are all successful in their own right.

A US Navy Veteran, Tiffany is sensitive and understanding of the special needs of our Armed Forces. She offers discounts to this special group of individuals and their families, not only to honor their service but also because of the kinship she feels with the military community.

www.soulcareonlinehypnosis.com

www.metaphysicalliving.com

Tiffany Ruiz, M.Msc.

Pop culture matters, But Why Tho? Hosts Kate, Adrian, and Tom answer why some parts of pop culture are talked about, remembered, rebooted, and loved. You can find them at:

http://butwhythopodcast.libsyn.com/

Made in the USA
Coppell, TX
16 November 2024

40337292R00066